KATE MILLER

The
Long Beds

CΛRCΛNET

First published in Great Britain in 2020 by
Carcanet
Alliance House, 30 Cross Street
Manchester M2 7AQ
www.carcanet.co.uk

Text copyright © Kate Miller 2020

The right of Kate Miller to be identified as the author
of this work has been asserted in accordance with the
Copyright, Designs and Patents Act of 1988; all rights reserved.

A CIP catalogue record for this book is
available from the British Library.

ISBN 978 1 78410 967 7

Cover image by Zephyr Penoyre
Book design by Andrew Latimer
Printed in Great Britain by SRP Ltd, Exeter, Devon

The publisher acknowledges financial
assistance from Arts Council England.

CONTENTS

THE LONG BEDS

to the keepers of the states of sleep, my nearest

And ye lie in me
And scarce dare move,
Lest earth and its love
Should fade away
Ere the full of the day.

– William Morris
poem for his bed at Kelmscott

and sometime voices
That, if I then had waked after long sleep,
Will make me sleep again.
– The Tempest

OUTSIDE THE MIND SHOP

Fox shrieks, it is the hour of fox
patrols between late taxis and dawn trucks.

Be not afeard, the night is full of noises.
Drowse and attune, like Caliban

when voices haunt him. My bed's an island
where I've *cried to dream again*

beside the ones who once lay close to me,
the nearest. If I could only sleep and hear them speak.

But in the dark outside the Mind Shop
foxes must be tearing into stuff

dropped off, unwanted, out of date.
Bits they disdain will end washed up

tomorrow in Tintagel Crescent, jetsam
of ill-fitting shoes, a sack of toys,

a bitten leather glove, inevitable baby clothes.
My mind is running on the trash they leave

mislaid or missed, matter once embraced
debased, the vixen uttering her screech.

LOCOMOTION OF LAUNDRY

All things began in order, so shall they end and so shall they begin again
– Sir Thomas Browne

Bedding, always being displaced, you could say
exiled, forms a line of bundles, refugees.
Cloth which wound around the living
 – and preserves the record in its creases –
only has to flop down on the floor
to forgo its old life.
              Sheets and towels must wait for their ablution,
taps to open, washer drum to turn.
      There's no hurry.
Everything is taken up and everything descends,
tugged from the rubber cervix, treated to a midwife's slap,
          each coming newly
                  into being at the separation.
In the tango of its hanging,
     a shirt or linen that until this morning bore
               another body's trace,
takes up position as a fighter, felon, dancer, tackler, striker,
air-blown along the line.
There may be occasional arrests
yet piece by piece they are reshaped,
redeemed in the perpetual lifting and laying-on of hands
and *so shall they begin again* to enter every room.

FLAG

I live by blue,   the island's air and waters:
blue answers to the prayers I say

As sunrise strips the white sheets off the sea
I start up hill   to hoist my country's colours,

a goat or chickens in my wake
God grant me this day liberty or death beneath the flag

Waves running
carry to me   the sea's *galanolefci*   blue striped with light

while out of Turkish waters   into Greek
       monk seals weave towards our shore

I've never wanted for a match for blue
God grant me this day   liberty or death

beneath the flag, the third and last one   Kostas brought,
          I used to spread it on our bed

I don't recall this little tear
Tonight I'll darn it   with white hairs from my plait

since now I'm out of thread
                   God grant me   this day

LANDING

In the night sea of our bed,
when I drift against your arm,
when I reach towards your hand
for anchorage,
                          my landing dream
recurs – not as in 'here I disembark'
but in the place with many doors ahead
on stairs away from home,
                                    unlit, with missing
treads. I lurch, I grab a newel post, feel for
an even floor.
                          Take comfort in the thought
of mooring… steady, jelly heart. The jetty,
jump ashore…
                          I would wave but your eye is on the sail.
Your right hand on the tiller shifts,
                                    uncouples,
frees the jib. And you're away and out there
in your dream you tack.

THE LONG BEDS

When we look out at dawn
across the shipyard, rafts are being fetched
by tugs, and on the rafts whole families have slept
out in the cool,

grand old dynastic families in white,
the women's faces veiled. Motionless
and queenly in repose, they're surely only playing dead?

Past floats
one part-unwrapped young person with a lovely face,
big eyes perhaps I recognise. In girlhood
wasn't she my closest friend?

Meanwhile attendants rouse the men-folk
bringing cups. And all the time the sea, dull green,
laps at their long beds hanging in the water.

THE QUARTERS

At the foot of the village abandoned last century
Notre Dame de la Porporière is locked shut
but the quarters are rung automatically. Two o'clock,
quarter past, half past two,

when a man lies awake through the hour he fears,
the closest he draws to the dark. When
he murmurs and cleaves to his wife
although she may not turn and she may not speak,

being sharp to the creatures of night,
to the silence of owls as they fish,
sailing the vineyard in waves. When
she senses the moment a shrew is swept up

or dropped on the bank of a field drain, when
the woodpile shifts to make space
for its hermit, a fire salamander. When
clouds clear, the sky is an upland of stars,

then ways from the house become rivulets
watered with moon spray, milkiest spattering,
and striped by the hulks of the fruit trees,
long dead, two horses are bathing in light.

KEEPERS OF THE STATES OF SLEEP AND WAKEFULNESS, FRAGMENT FROM A MASQUE

– after THE SECOND MASQUE *by Ben Jonson*

> *Here, a Curtain was drawn (on which the* Night *was painted),*
> *Paper (treated with Fantex, antimicrobe/biocidal, flame*
> *retardant) pleated Blue, which served to screen a* Patient...
> *and the* Scene *discover'd... a small* Cell *by Moonlight;*
> *in the midst thereof a fitful Sleeper on an ingeniously configur'd Bed.*
> *At which attended eight* Figures, *representing* Keepers
> *of the States of* Sleep *and* Wakefulness. *The first, AYINKA*

IN a Robe of *thunder*-colour; her crazy hair, a Circle of Crows before Cloud;
In her hand a paper cup, with two *Pills*, a *white*, a *red*. Then came *PRISCILLA*

IN a garment of *sky*-colour, with a *Mist white* plastic apron about her waist:
on her Face a mask and in her Hand an ear thermometer. The third was *DIGNA*

IN indigo, with *blue-violet* gloves, like Aconites: upon a Blood-test tray,
vials, cannulas and cotton swabs, a Tourniquet. There followed *ELEANOR*

IN divers hues of *Silver, Iron* and *Tin,* her *Gold* Hair loosing pins, she pans
the contents of the catheter bag; her eyes turned up and smiling. Fifth, *CHERYL*

IN one Hand *Agilia*, the IV drip stand, in the other a fat Pouch of *Ciprofloxacin.*
Her Temple bears a childhood scar, her talk harks of Trinidad. The sixth *SOFIA*

IN a *Cherry* cardigan, hair plaited like a Raspberry round her Head. She tugs
the Cable of a monitor, *Welch Allyn Vital Signs,* her dance partner. Next *RAMATU*

IN *Pitch*-dark Robe and pale mask, her Buskins black and weighty, rubber soled;
In her gloved Hands the dull blue cuff and pressure Bulb. And last *AMOR*

A Personage whose State and Air of calm had something of all these who kept her Company and something more. On her Breast a *heart*-shaped Watch; in her Hand a lighted *Torch*.

AMOR

ALL Horrors vanish, and all Name of *Death*,
Be all Things here as calm as is my Breath.

Here she led a Dance so curious it cannot be
describ'd again by any Art save that of their
own footing, for which the Patient, who could
remain silent no longer, entreated them thus.

SONG

Refresh me with your Names like Flowers
Ayinka, Priscilla, Digna, Eleanor
Cheryl, Sofia, Ramatu, Amor,
Stepping through the Night each Hour

You wear your Names like Constellations
Ayinka, Priscilla, Digna, Eleanor
Cheryl, Sofia, Ramatu, Amor,
Wake me with your observations

Refresh me with the Names I grow to love
Cheryl, Sofia, Digna, Eleanor
Ramatu, Priscilla, Ayinka, Amor,
Splendid masquers in your pansy petal gloves
with Names like Flowers I grow to love

At which they danc'd again to the Eccho of their names

WHY THE FARM LAY EMPTY

A gecko flattens
through a crack. The walls are bare
but for three Holy Marys sharing
the dingy light with one small photo,
framed: the boys in Sunday best,
solemn, sallow, five and eight.

In winter it was Diego's job
to mind the herd, bring them in at dusk
and pen them in the rubble shed
that leaned against the wall outside this room
where he and Alejandro had their little beds.

In summer when the goats were on the hill,
the brothers slept out on the threshing floor,
sprawled below the axle of the cart of stars,
that spans the Milky Way. On ticklish straw,
they woke to meteor showers flung
across the Hunter's path.

One stellar harvest night
Alejandro went off his head, took a sickle
to the insect bites that swelled his feet
inside the tight shoes he had worn to Mass.
It was the summer he first shaved,
solemn, moon-faced, mute.

COMING TRUE FROM SEED

Your cousins sent a handful in a twist of bubble-wrap
        the Autumn you were born. Each little armoured cap
            held contradictions, offers to the touch:
the dimpling of a thimble and the stubby pin of a grenade:
            made to cradle and release a small smooth head.

In Spring I noticed that one acorn meant
        to stand its ground, stay put, as any small child would,
            and so it anchored up and down in earth,
through earth, by sticking out two tongues of growth
            from tarnished halves of brass.

Antenna poking from the grass became the first line of a tree
        – lengthening – the hedgers' *whip*, upright and thin,
            gaining in girth... until the end of a fifth winter when twigs began
to open to the sky from fists of buds, gloved hands
            sporting mussel-orange cuffs of curly leaves.

Fifteen years it takes until a new oak
        gets its maiden crop and maybe fifteen more before the seed sets true.
            One year when you're grown, you'll roll
a clutch of green-skinned acorns, phials in your palm,
            next generation to the seeds which rattled down

upon the roof in wind and frost, the way they fell
        the night your grandfather gave up the ghost beneath the oak
            presiding like a strong brown grizzled god
above his bed. We laid him where you were conceived,
            his resting place, your start, inside the oak-leaved earth.

OUTNUMBERED, ONE BY ONE

Here lies my child, full-grown,
half buried in the sand, his legs still
warm but as the sun gives in
to ocean, ever more inert.

The wind is freshening.
The sounds of coastal life
diminish in proportion to the cool.
I shuffle closer to him on his bed of sand.

At home I'd fit beside him,
counting him to sleep: just recitation
soothed him. He loved numbers,
their repeating scale.

In the hope he'd nod off,
I would slow – anticipating
separation – leaving intervals,
the fading of a song

extending into
silence

                    *

*

Stars
just waiting to be called
peek out all over the Pacific's dome
and Joe Breeze calls their names.

At every name he gives
I feel a prickling of my skin.
How come you know so many stars? we ask.

They haven't changed, he says, since Grandpa
schooled him standing in the yard
counting them by eye. Only when Joe knew
the hundred nearest

would the old man introduce
remote ones with a telescope.
And now we see, as he did, deep
streams, deep tracks through star-snow,

landscapes of star-seeded fields.
Those distances bear seams of light,
a little of the infinite. The silk roads
run in our direction. Always towards.

Some stars are jittery and shy.
As they approach, they reach for us
and we are bound, two Gullivers together
tied and netted on the beach.

KNAPSACK OF PARTING GIFTS

Where you are going next
time is not watched. You'll find a store of hours
without clocks: time to fix
the boat – although an offshore breeze no sooner
sensed, you'll have the sail un-reefed,
be heading for the islands –

time to leaf through books you thought were lost,
or cook the morning's catch of trout
outside your boyhood tent.
Here's marmalade, home-made, since breakfast
in the afterlife may not be up to scratch.
And do you recognise the knife?

The picnic knife which skidded
on the waxy paper grocers wrap round cheese
and toppled thirty feet sheer down a wall in Rome
to fall in nettles in an orchard that you tracked
by the vaguest *Blue Guide* map,
stole into by an unlocked gate – you brought it back.

We had time then.
Already full, this weather-beaten bag,
I wish I could have packed more in.

THE QUEEN OF NAPLES, ASKED ABOUT HER CHILDHOOD HOME

It had no name, no proper trees
(our fires were built of lumber washed from wrecks).
Uncharted and unclaimed except by Cal who called it his
Bee Isle. A touch of Ustica,

same burnt volcanic rocks
with tunnels, caves and underwater scratchy shelves
where phosphorescence, streaming in
at night, anointed sea anemones and spangled urchins.

Same teeming fish and curious young gulls
neglecting nothing, picking over
sea-stripped finds, rag and bone, fisheyes.

Same climate, harsh – almost too dry
for birds. Father would stand
above the beach to welcome huge migrating flocks.
They dived and fell like grain on dust.

Same restless airs, a sort of sighing in the scrub,
the swish of lizards scuttling to cracks
and always the *continuo*, till dark, of native bees...

I used to go with Cal and, climbing to their nest
(so agile then, I was a marmoset) I'd stay suspended
in a cleft of stone, hours on baking afternoons
I should have been at rest.

And what Cal didn't know
of bees, the Reverend Butler's treatise later showed.
(That in the hive there is no king; instead

a female, fed to fullness, fanned by workers' wings,
grows grand, emboldened, loud. And ready
to assume the mantle of her colony, how noisily
she stakes her claim to *Monarchie*).

If then I heard the descant of a piping bee,
her challenge to the older queen to move her swarm,
instinctively I left the nest alone.

The time I had to shoo him off, Cal only wanted me,
with my small hands, to steal honeycomb.
So close we came to blows, the bees were roused,
a thousand eyes and *twangling instruments*

chastised and we were stung,
each pinch more stinging, blinded by their wild black storm
which hid our island from the sun and rained upon it

shining men. Who wooed me from my father's cell
with promises of fountains, avenues of trees,
hunting, harvest, gilded carriages, the gas blue fires
of their volcano. I asked if I might ride a horse,

keep birds. Would there be bees on banks of flowers
I had seen in dreams? They did not say
their queen, weighted down with cloth, stiffened with baleen,
rarely ventured in the sun.

You know the noise the wind makes
coming at you over grass? How it buffets
the box of your head, loud as the sea, so loud you can't think
what the memory is.

        Until one afternoon - there's no wind
and the common is cracking with drought - a second sound,
the scuffle of a brittle leaf, recalls acutely the harsh tick
tick tick of holm oaks in a line – leaves crimped and clicking
as they marked the time - in summer
on a different common.

        The slim brown leaf's a plectrum
picking at a string. Insisting *Hurry, child*
past tennis courts, a bowling green, Lord Nelson on his plinth,
salt-glazed sea-view hotels.

        Child! See the shapes sounds make,
pommelled, connecting like jigsaw bits, sounds shaping you
as you work at the puzzle, putting each piece into place,
finding the difficult fit.

        Come to a halt
in a sitting room furnished from India turn of the century,
yellow with roses, a cage of canaries, pot pourri,
papers and reading glass. Near the desk
where your grandmother writes you're pretending to read
about kings. In Muriel's hand is her pen
and the slim brown leaf is her nib.

WOMAN OF LETTERS

On the blotter, splotched, an envelope lies slit
by sun or with the old brass paper-knife,
an interruption in the gloom. Where's the letter
– and from whom? I vow to read her secret life.

We know the correspondence she posts out
to family, her missives to the press, much less
about the yellow papers tied with binding tape
and locked up in the chest. Rifling for a treasury tag

I come across a scarlet Silvine book
with carbon leaves, page after tattooed page,
the log (eventually I learn) she keeps – with dates –
of publishers' polite rejection slips.

The lid is off a heavy jar of spider leggy ink.
I wait to see her free those spiders when she writes
her wiry black left-handed script. They run
amok across the sheets.

INVITATION TO THE WORD GAME

Let's make our way out of the everyday
how-now. We're looking for a lamp-lit table
with two well-worn armchairs and, yes,
an ancient sponge-bag like a flattened brain.
It holds a rubble of tongues. Serve each
a clutch of seven capitals, jumbled
tiles of memory we'll sort to play.

SPEAKING VOICE

I

English was her mother tongue but her singsong
was made in India. It had a travelling rise and fall
with which she spurred on compound words,
run-a-<u>way</u>, roc-<u>king</u>-horse, <u>rail</u>-way <u>train</u>.

Broadcasting on 'Children's Hour'
and 'Woman's Hour' (those days the wire-less)
she almost did sound English born and bred.
Yet when she spoke of India as *the house*

where she was born or sometimes as *the friend*
whose *house* it was, the audience imagined
she was not. Hindustani words strayed
into tales she told: names of trees and jungle birds,

dairy cows her mother milked, game,
gymkhana trophies, Indian sweets, flowers.
She learned a secret to the art
of storytelling: always smile while speaking:

encouraged by her *ayah* or Mukkah
the *shikari* with a winking eye, half-blind
crackshot who took her brother hunting
and could spin a sportsman's yarn.

In her narrating voice you heard her smile.

2

After India, she came 'home'
but in the London Blitz, her home was lost
the night her small flat took a direct hit.
Nothing left intact except the bed

buried among bricks and fallen books.
She later told us her recurring dream – no smile
would soften it – of being struck dumb
as she came on a ragged line of chancers

scrabbling in the dust, cramming
her cutlery and clothes into a pillowcase.
She tried to shout but no words formed.
A voice she didn't recognise as hers cried *giddhon,*

the word the village children shrieked,
running as a pack, drumming sticks… *giddhon,*
at huge birds strutting on a corpse washed up along
the Ganges, *giddhon,* you vultures, get down, get down, get down.

I slept once in that bed beside
a wharf of papers from the worlds she travelled in
between the wars. After a welcome of few words,
a dose of brandy for the out-of-sorts,
she sat me on her turned-down single bed,
the curtains pulled against a dazzling afternoon.
Green folds silenced what we might have said.

Twenty hours on... I drew them back,
a hint of camphor in the velvet but no sign of her,
except outside, the bed of spiky dahlias
supposed to whirl in fire-wheels
like flowers of childhood in Bengal
she claimed were so big, so densely grown
you never saw their stems.

Austere the light, the room, the narrow bed
I lay in to untie her writing case, unfold
telegrams, dry snips of type,
a child sent abroad, reports of missing, dead,
love declared, love scorned – in tiny script –
an envelope 'NOT KNOWN AT THIS ADDRESS',
her story & my father's & his father's
before him, the long warp lines of ink.

EARLIEST POEM IN WHICH MURIEL FIGURES

By the lake at Naini Tal
when Muriel went to school
the dormitory was often cold,
the summer months were cool.

No aeroplane climbed upwards
in her sky of gentian blue:
every leaf and every cloud
the gods let drop was new.

Muriel comes from *myrrh* or *muir gheal* (Gaelic) sea-bright.
The eyes (*Nain*) of Sati fell from the sky into this lake (*Tal*).

SCHOOL PRIZE, 1912

The Poetical Works of Elizabeth Barrett Browning, bound in snakeskin

Her father never spoke of sea-going, or took her
to the coast. Just upped and booked
his passage to Australia. Ten years a boarder
in a convent in the Himalayas

and with advice from Sister Anne
she chose this book to show her sea and foreign
landscapes she might never know. And even now
her prize falls open at 'The Seaside Walk' or 'The Sea Mew'.

Reading of the moon-swung tide, salt water's
stranger moods, of shifts and distances, the way
the sea lays siege to shore, small wonder that she gained
an ear for how waves strafe a cliff or waltz

with sand or soothe a troubled beach,
an eye for what air builds above the sea:
marshalling yards and sprawling
camps of cloud, storm factories.

ALBUM WITHOUT PHOTOGRAPHS

1   *Empty Frame*

Without a face
or arms (it framed

my parents
frozen in a pose

in a Calcutta studio,
then my beau

in uniform)
my sentinel,

whose blankness
serves to shield

me (from sight)
as I have guarded it

at the going
down of the sun

and in the morning,
in and out of trunks and through the Blitz.

Cucumber moon, the merest sliver,
a dozing fan-puller and my mother
at the bungalow in mounting heat
before the coming of the rains.
                              Unsettled
                  by a frantic dog, she rises
heavy to her feet — around her lantern insects
swarm — while on the dark verandah, something living
easing from a roll of matting,
                        passes with a sweep like a sharpened
scythe. *Memsahib, saanp, saanp!*
                              Her lamplight swerves
            below her belly, down along a length of snake.
In reach of her, the cobra

                              rears
                                erect,
                              gold eyes
                              fastened on
                                        her
                              bulk,
                                  black
                              hood
                                  flared –
                                        black
                                        flame

                              wavers,

                              bows.
                                        My mother
                  falls to earth. The waters break.

3   *My Other Country*

At twilight Mother leaves with milk and quinine
for the village. Father's gone up-river with my brother
after a black crocodile, man-eater they say,
struck a washerwoman yesterday. I feed the crane
in Mother's aviary and pet the dogs, avoiding
Father's caged hyena. If only he'd teach me
to ride and shoot I could do more than read
about our Queen and Country in my hideout
up the guava tree. Speckled books show
castles, lochs and orchards, churches, village greens.
The sleepy Ganges barely stirs. I dream of open
water, naval harbours. My dream fleets reach
ports where streets with real pavements lead
to hospital, a bobby on the beat, a lighted library.

4   *Bouquet*

My beau, as fine an officer as you could ask,
fell with the Old Contemptibles in France.
At weddings, when the new bride went away,
I'd always rear to catch the bright bouquet
and then I'd dance the young under the table
in efforts to forget how my love led me to the stables,
murmuring *my beauty*, tongue-clicking in my hair
as if he were the groom and I his mare.
Picked flowers have for me the tack-room scent
of saddlery and liniment.

5   *My Highland Wedding & No Bouquet*

1 May 1920, Northern India, now Pakistan

I wore a dress the durzee ran up overnight.
Silk as pale as lassi. My bouquet
was due from Rawalpindi with the groom
who'd drive the forty miles to Murree.
Instead I had to hold my dog tight
in my arms, in case she bit the minister.
Still Sandy didn't appear, nor his best man.
Their car and flowers had come to grief en route;
saved by the weekly postal van, he raced,
kilt skewing, to the kirk in time to claim
his bride. The dog leaned out and nipped his hand.
The minister, who played the bagpipes on
a short walk to the manse, was quick to serve
a better nip – of Scotch – and we were cheered
to see our cake was tied in Gordon tartan
ribbon with a spray of heather, dried
to white. The heat a hundred by midday.

6   *No Monsoon*

Sent home from India, my first encounter
with a kettle and a kitchen range, I earned the slur

handless, no good with your hands,
intoned by dour Scottish aunts.

One day the docks at Tilbury - the train,
the dismal lines of back to backs

the next, the rain, all afternoon, all night –
genteel rain – no smashing to the ground,

no burning, no monsoon. No thunder.
I watched grass wait politely

through the wee hours: green throats
opened only slightly,

teetotal, they're not thirsty.
Their small smiles revealed poor teeth of mud.

Curtains stirred in a teacup wind,
tut tutted at the milkman's splash.

The aunts went out galoshed from door to door all day
on *kirk work*, eking out a pinch of Indian tea.

7   *After the Frontier, 'the Golden Road to Samarkand'*
   Afghanistan, 1923

White stones marked the Durand Line. A soldier
waved us through and we were leaving India behind
forever, first British family to cross that year.
I clutched my sickly child as we passed the train:
two hundred camels nose to tail: the car so out of place
it was invisible. Wound down the window, sniffed
fleece, sandalwood, asafoetida, a whiff of gunpowder.

Armed traders clanked alongside
kith and kin. Donkeys loped beneath old women,
small girls cradled hens, nursing mothers swayed, eyes low.
Habitual travellers, they knew the season not the date;
a herders' track was all the land they'd ever take.
At evening stars poked straws through sky
to drain the day's heat from the rocks. Roadside
campfires of the caravanserais lit faces so lined
surely some were known to Abraham.

The long past beamed across the night
in lantern slides, holy scenes. I saw them bow their heads,
intent on something shared. A waking
baby's lifted hands.

MYRRH

Unclasped, the swollen writing case disperses
aerogrammes, faint leaves, air blue. But fainter,
sweeter than the smell of hide, another find tips out,

the egg-shaped phial we children coveted. It incubated
in the delicate glass-sided and glass-lidded
kidney table, among small treasures from the East.

Dark green cut glass so champagne-bottle thick
the tiny flask turned emerald
if ever she permitted us to twirl it to the light.

And since the silver cap has flipped
wide open on its handmade hinge,
it yields the scent of myrrh, her myrrh released,

a long-held last breath
rising from the mossy cloth and paper nest.

IN THE DUTCH TRADITION

when a person died, black cloth was draped
across all views to guard
the roaming soul from venturing outside.

She didn't hold with this idea.
So she chose one large picture: Connemara

on a good day, windless, treeless, grassy, dry,
a stretch of country she had never seen.
This graced the room she sat in going blind
for over twenty years, a mild sunlit scene

above the unlit space where her old head would rest.
The seeing soul… she thought its last
initiative should be to launch and fare
forward unencumbered into salt-bright, sea-bright air.

NOW MAY I ARISE

Come in, come in, at last you're here
        to spring me from my foggy English cell.
Now my eyes are rested, I can just make out
        your caterpillar mouthparts nipping at the dark,
sawing a ragged line of light along the edges of the blind.

You've left a fringe of petals, guava maybe
        and I'm still in the half-light of the guava tree
I'd climb so Mother wouldn't see me on her evening drive,
        the scent of horse and watered violets rising from below.
        Let's creep out together

emerging larvae from the throats of flowers. Help me up
        up up a slope of alpine blue, blue as gentian,
through the Himalayan meadows where the bearers bore me
        swaying in a *dandy* to a place the reverend sisters told me
        meant in Hindi lake of eyes.

All these years I've dreamed of a return
        to brightness, folded in
the pleated white of Choti-ayah's spotless sari, patted, hushed
        … quick now, this old room is shrinking …
        at a distant gateway barking dogs fall quiet.

One star's left to light the sandbanks on the Ganges.
        Must we leave so early? Is it Sunday, the long ride
to church? Swaddled, bundled in the *tonga,*
        we are starting out at dawn,
        the jungle waking, our two white bullocks racing.

(HER ENVOI) A CHIDING

First bird sounds the alarm.
Wake up! Leaf tips unscroll,
curves of crocus swell.
Stand up straight, flower! Keep still
while I brush your hair – don't flop.
Now! Grow up
because here comes
the long-winter-months man
with a worm; he'll want you
back beside him in the warm
of his dried brown mattress.
There you'll stay
kept and you will have to lie
in wait another year
if ever you're to rise, my sweet,
white from the starred field,
eager as the sun.

REACH

A cry stiffens
                  the pool's skin. Listen – still dark –
we lumber from the mud and dead reed
                                    dip of riverbank.
        Thin slip of wind
                          puts on a little flesh,
        stirs the stream.
                          Blow, wind, cheers a bird, shake
the stream awake, show her your violet streak!
                                    Send her downriver to rinse
            in the breath-warmth of creatures,
                                    vole-squeak, cow-sigh,
                          swish of a heron
        shifting heddle feet.
                          About a branch an eddy
            flips glass hair of willow.
                          Water holds a smeary mirror up
                                    to tips of light.
I'm keeping one eye
            on the boat while Blanche sets out my paints.
                          My other eye
                                    is climbing into space to reach
                          by stairs of cold, spires
            topping the air's cliffs of ice.
    As birdsong rises,
                as water winds, is winched upwards
                          in the screw of poplars,
        as vapour lifting to a clearing sky
                is gathered in the net,
we mark each break   in the mesh of morning
            mended with wires of light.

FIRST FLOWER OF THE DAY

I

hesitating

like a woman before morning
hesitating to be up and dressed,
a poppy's yet to shuck its wrap,

the bud held
low and hooded in a dull green cap.

Stray hairs stick out stiff as whiskers
on the neck, crookneck,
demurring to the weight of bud.

Instruments of light are lifted,
hover over opened and half open flowers,

pause above this drowsy patient,
papaver somniferum, tagged, prepped - but not so fast,

take your time, *papaver*, in delivering,
slowly present
the swell beneath pale stretchmarks, giving way

the sepal case unclasps

2

about ten minutes, all it takes
to happen without sound, no snap, sigh, gasp,
mere separation at the pursed lines, lips

part and through the sheath a tongue of pale purple slips,
reveals a crease, a sucked thin frill

stained pinkish white, already bleaching,
colour bleeding inwards to the crush of tissue

3

Just as a woman then – at daybreak –
considers and shakes out her clothes,
this flower lets out long white tucks.

A double Z
along the folds from tip to base
unzips. Air dries and edges cockle

so when sun enters by the opened slits
that first archaic reddish flush seeps up
inside the flower's still secret spot.

Light mops up the salt-blued wine
while un-cramped petal hems
balloon, float slightly crisping in the flow of air.

They curl and bell… *to airy thinness beat*…
shaping's slow but slower yet is filling out,
attaining fullness, flaring into space

a half hour poised (late stage) upon the very
edge of patency

medusa's fluid dance meets parachute

4

Mignonne, allons … Ronsard appeals to a girl
to contemplate the rose *qui ce matin avait déclose*
sa robe de pourpre au soleil

but how unlike his sturdy rose, exuding
glamour in a sumptuous dress, sun-kissed,

the poppy is – within a day or two, the long June day,
her petals wilt to mauve or fall. The weather
strips her down to working parts.

Look properly inside, *Mignonn*e: she may be faded
but not finished yet,

her heart's a crowded stadium,

a pompommed twirl where, middle of the pitch,
already amber stamens, all male,

form a scrum of anthers to contest
who plays the pistil's glistening ball.

                    the room, a room of rain,
June's loaded rain, the roses dashed, a river running
down the glass, so much for guttering. Inside it pearls
the walls, brims over like Tarkovsky's rain
dissolving frames. The mirror blurs

                          is this the deluge
in the workshop where they waded to the sound of water
filling, pausing at the edge of vessels, spilling
– no, that was by torchlight (though the fall and rise
of rain was something he returned to over and again,
examining its onset, rhythms)

                        is it the café
in the downpour they were caught in when her hair
streamed and the books got soaked. *Better ditched*
he said, since *felted pages never come unstuck enough*
for reading. No reading would explain
how water sought a route through everything,
wearing a desire path of rain

                      and – just as then
her trouser legs and sleeves behaved like wicks
in plant experiments by bearing water up her limbs
to make her bloom – re-entering with him
                    the room, a room of rain

SALVAGE

In years gone by and now again
the river's docile
tributaries swell, topple

banks like heifers clashing in the lane.
Hide-heavy water bodies fall
on fields of flood.

At the foot of walls
the turning waters leave
a mess of mirrors, puddle deep,

to show the ruined
complexion of the clouds
to one who sifts,

lifts broken branches or a gate to free
strayed geese, the buoyant
coop, a broody hen.

PRESENCE

Before the bell for prayer
a lad dropped shoeless from a tree-limb
to lead her through the wood.
She used to think it was an ordinary wood.

From out of flicker-architecture –
from the flame and spin of leaf-fall –
where aisles were evergreen, where sacristy and lady
chapel stood, screened by yew or polished holly,
figures would appear.

When, in an oak, she saw
the fingers of a penitent revealed
by sunset, in a glow of apple-jellied light,

her eye went from the joined hands
ridged with bark, across the torso
clothed in hair, carved
like water coursing to the ground,

the coursing lignified, down
to bony ankles and the toes,
exposed and burnished roots.

When in rain she found
a kneeler, emerald with starry moss,
at the apostle feet of twinned tree trunks,
she recognised the brothers,
black robes water-sheened.

They tested her: she answered
she had come to know them
by their hands and feet.

Again the shock-head angel
passed her, running in a pale vest.
His bare feet, muscled, earthy –
real enough, she thought –
thudded on leaf-mould matting.

That he was sent, she did not doubt.

UNWRAPPING
from The Sack

When the dark glass river wormed
with barges dragging out the dirt-cold dead
she broke into a long box, after coin.

Just as soldiers quartered in a country church
saw only firewood when they smashed the screens,
so the cold lent power to her arm.

Three stiff parcels lay inside, sealed,
a sweetish trace of myrrh, silk thread
easily unwound, spilled slack.

If superstitious
she would have left the parcels well alone,
gloved in river-bitten skin. Nor would she trust

her eyesight (since the last cathedral,
lightless even at noon). Old finger-bones – in sainted
hands – she told herself, wear rings.

The city has two byelaws all citizens must learn when they are toddlers, never written or displayed. The first is silence: silence in all public places, including café tables out of doors, on benches in the squares, consensual silence where one can root and grow. After three weeks going to and fro, still wondering what the second is, she is on the bus and sees a man she feels she knows. Bird eyed, neat beard, a little like Paul Klee. They sit in the familiar, far from gloomy pocket of no talking demanded by the law. At her stop, he breaks the hush with 'Let the heart go fishing'. Everyone looks up. 'You come', says he, 'all eyes and ears, as foreigners who love this city always do. Allow yourself to wait. Each day exerts its pull, defines. No day without a line.' Hands her a book. She holds his eye but dares not speak. Jumps free, the bus clanks on. Grey cover, nothing on the spine. At first glance, every page is blank. Slinking through the flower market she shields the book from droplets running off the foliage, under the surprised expressions of giant greenhouse pansies. Lays it like a bible in the library and turns the pages slowly, willing it to reveal a key, a turned down corner, erratum slip. Blank, blank, blank… no, wait… releasing from the paper, diffused and then intense, the smells of parks in autumn rise: crushed grass, chrysanthemum, wild marjoram, the browner stink of bombsites: oxeye daisy, burnt bedding, shit and, whoa, what is that? – crab? Scents lift as if she's stumbled in them walking. Monkish at dim lit desks, bowed over texts, heads tilt up, necks extend, noses wrinkle, lips open to shape a strange intake of breath, part exclamation part Mona Lisa smile. And every face is known to her, a lined and grown up version of the face of children from the blasted city she grew up in.

A MAN WALKS INTO THE SEA

There's the man in the striped gown.
Same time every morning he tramps the shingle barrow,
reads his watch, removes it, stripping down,
dips and tests and slips in through the slapping shallows.

Today an onshore southsoutheasterly
cooks the water to a boil of jam, frothing yeastily.
Can't help thinking Le Corbusier, who swam alone
each day, as this man does, was drowned.

Over the beach go herring gulls, a thick-set couple,
a girl whose trainers sink in pebbles as she jogs,
dog walker, pipe-smoker, all oddly uniform in purple
fleece – except the prancing dog.

Landlubber noises off: the backing refuse cart, continuous
peep, car alarm or hedge bird spat: until a snatch of sunlight
makes two cyclists' Lycra gleam fish-sinuous,
a woman hallowed, floating by in white.

What is anticipation? The man who takes to water
sets the temper of the day, more telling than barometer
and clock. I clamber on a chair to scan the bay: far off, a speck...
I brighten – I missed you, brave soul, welcome back.

A PIECE OF CHALK

*But though I could not with a crayon get the best out of the landscape,
it does not follow that the landscape was not getting the best out of me.*
– G.K. Chesterton

I long to be on the Downs
and I will take my lead from Chesterton, setting off
one splendid morning blue and silver, a pocket stuffed
with coloured chalks, a pocket knife he calls his *infant sword*
and a papoose of parcel paper from the kitchen drawer
because he likes the rough-and-ready brown – *primeval
or poetical* – suited to the new day of creation
with its yeasty odour of *October woods or beer*.

He warns
Do not imagine I was going to sketch from Nature.

No, he is on a quest for mystical, heraldic and symbolic
beasts, *old gods*, a fiery flock of stars.
He draws a regal animal in purple: she shines
with seven horns: he manifests her soul and mystery.

I am after visions too. No simple cow should be allowed
to hold my eye. This isn't about scenery
except a glimpse perhaps – the pale green sea, the crowns
of far off trees – oceanic and processional.

And on the skyline he and I are blessed.
For with the penknife it is soft enough to prise a chunk,
a piece of chalk that is *the rock, the land itself* – where boundless
white surrounds us, a shrine, basilican,
aisle after aisle, rack upon rack,
an immense warehouse of white.

He is delighted by the way the mineral
in his hand has come to light from underground,
the sense the landscape works on him
and not the other way around,

– that's what I want. To be subject
to the underlying chalk, accept the almost tidal pull
that tugs me to the hill.

I mean to cross the *swell of living turf,*
be granted what the downland
grants to him, its queenly sweep of air and earth and light,

to halt before the pomp and glory of that loft
above the chalk, a whitening space, the place
you feel the power whiteness has

when white outdoes and gathers
force and leaps

upwards out of earth – white burning
haloes at the edge of dust in sunlight,
on leaves of grass, on ruts, on snail shells,
white arcing off the filaments of harebells –
to live on the illuminated page.

CLAIM

I call this plot my earth – no person
near – a scrap of field, my bowl of sky. In hard frost
everything has points like knives, the knife-blades
laid through whitened crumbs, grass a confection
of crackle, very late sweet peas fragile as glass.

I cut the last few bluish flowers, unknot
netting, stack the canes, reasoning they're not
too worn to come in handy one more season. I ought
to practice thrift as part of husbandry.
Until I sense another eye

light on me, lovat blue,
the colour of December air, a pair of narrowed eyes
aslant in coal black canthi. You never step
on no-man's land, inside the ring you like
to put – only ten feet – between us.

Natty in your ginger gangster suit, you hint
at business, Fox: some contraband
stashed here in a hoary pile of hay.
Ears swivel to the heap, all vigilant
because … I might, what? Loot?

Slouch off then, feign nonchalance,
you won't go hungry! Loop back, break into
trot. I wish I had your nose for new material,
your instinct to corral your stock.
My gathering is archival, yours, survival.

A BIRD DOES NOT SING BECAUSE IT HAS AN ANSWER
– Chinese proverb

Sylvie has stayed out all night for weeks in search of roosts.
Alert to early jostlings, on her haunches in a beechwood
she's matching *teek-a-teek-a*
                              fu phew fu ee yeu – yee yeu
        in electronic shorthand. Technically
a whizz, she's been inventing
ring-tones on a cell-phone since the nineties.

That's not the hard bit; now to perfect an app
to locate the territorial – and arboreal – zones
the cockbirds claim to own, starting calling before dawn.

She has translated *tik-at, tsi-tsi-tsi,*
tikat tsi tikat tsi-tsi but she's stuck on *a-wa, Ah! wha .. awa!*   *hooo, who?*
                    spacy and euphonious,

                              the sudden brash alarm of TSEEP
TSEEP and a sneezing TSEUT
        followed by a little *tseep*, then the hurried *uppa uppa, uppa
pew*, which keeps Sylvie on her toes; she wants to factor in
breath taking and the pause,
                              the pause   the pause
for sunrise, the falling mute, a little shuffling on the twigs
                    (the trees put on their gloves of light)
Sylvie gilded, head cocked birdlike, waiting for the first
hen to break her silence.

WATERLOO SUNRISE

I

If you have passed this way at sunrise, you'll know
it happens in a kind of blue, a fade through blotted blues,
l'heure bleue, which glimmers for an hour or so,
while London turns towards it. Towers abrupt as tree stumps
purple first, contrails – swallow tailed – shine.
The river's still. And bridges like dray horses stand in line
for hitching to the day's long load of light.

When birds, disputing what the morning says to do,
fall quiet – listen – wait for wingbeat,
footfall, trundle, gear change, cough… a little breeze
picks up, a warm touch on the lip of rails, sweet
on the pouts of dolphin lamp posts.

You're at a point which juts into the Thames,
where there have been three bridges over time,
granite, steel, concrete,
                              stays that laced and tightened
Lambeth to the Strand, each reducing what was once the stage
for scenes of river passage with their wood and water sets,
plots, noises off.
                    So in the build of sound are other strains,
not just today's: a creak and slop at slipways,
pontoons a-bob like Venice. Voices raised and voices
dropped, the pleasure garden crowds'
hubbub, curses, shouts and horns of watermen,
wet rope, slow splash of bodycatchers' oars,
tide's suck and slap.

Here on the southern approach at Waterloo
where station, church and churchyard have withstood
their share of losses and goodbyes,
I call on witnesses, come forward. Tell us, early risers,
what the sunrise heralded, what a day it was, a time.

11   *When I Call On Claude Monet*

He waves his arms and smokes. Gestures, doesn't speak
much English, doesn't like to talk. Eight weeks
he spends at the Savoy, a new hotel close by the bridge,
eats well (because the chef is French). The upper rooms he takes
are good. Equips one as his studio. Gets up at dawn to work.
This time of year that's touching six o' clock.

'I want to paint the air the bridge fits in, the envelope.'
His morning subject's usually
in coloured fog. But it can let him down:
the 3rd of Feb. 1901 he wrote to Alice:
Sunday, not a wisp of fog, and naturally no factory smoke.
Up came the sun, so dazzling I couldn't see a thing
against the Thames lit up all gold. God, it was beautiful,
the sun and its reflections very fine. I worked till nine,
in frenzy, four paintings begun.
(In place of breakfast, cigarettes.)

Two winter visits on, he's home at Giverny, completing
work on forty-one of these fog-clouded, cliff edge views.

He has us search along, above, beyond,
before, beneath. Out there to factory chimneys, docks,
here traffic into town: Covent Garden carts and cabs,
gigs, buses full of hats, gas lamp-lit queues,

while down beside the middle arches of the bridge
craft push like heavy fish.

The little garden bridge he's built across his ponds
is one sole curve, one span,
one rounded reach through space.

It lifts the floating world to meet the eye,
water flowers to reflected cloud.
It clasps the light of water to the light of sky.

What matters? Not the bridge itself but what it shapes.
Fusing eye and mind with place.

III   *Certain Figures Go Unrecorded*

After the Great War almost did away with horses,
the nine arched Georgian bridge which Monet watched
began to fail under the weight of wheels,
commuters, motor-driven loads.

In 1924 a bridge of steel relieved the flow.
Two generations standing in the river
side by side – the old in gradual decline –
a decade of dispute till the first 'unbuilding' blow
was struck, Midsummer, 1934.

Stone by stone and strut by strut, the old one was unpicked,
its trussed steel stand-in taking traffic south,
tiered with footways, cabling, gantries, derricks,
chutes which slid a hundred thousand tons of spoil
to waiting barges.

Displacement on the river, in the air.
Only then a new design: five concrete arches, sleek and white
as gulls' wings: began to rise in summer 1939.

The first year it was touch and go, most of the young
men got called up. Bomb damage in the Blitz,
eight local hits, (one at St John's), supplies were cut,
and females joined the labour force.
                                    Outdoors all day
while there was natural light, they travelled to and fro
to Waterloo in blackout,
sometimes neck and neck with sunrise. Clock on,
change into siren suits and toe-capped boots.
Instead of breakfast, cigarettes.

Though later no official mention's made,
no record kept of parts uncounted women played,
these were the "ladies" of the bridge.

IV *April 1944*

Meet Dorothy, Miss Robertson,
repurposer of steel. The Daily Herald says, *girl
welder aged 19*. She was a girl, a schoolgirl, when the war began.
I find her in the breaker's yard beside the bridge approach.

She dabs smuts off her face, a visor pushed up high, her crown.
Consults a mirror, which she keeps inside her ID card.
A ring on her right hand, enormous cowhide
gauntlets on her bench. Hammer, welding rod, electric leads.

So this is what the 'lady' does: dismantles and redeems
the steel: specialist 'make do and mend':
the phrase pops up in magazines.
She's in a team of three, her gaffer's Mrs May, her mate is June.

An inch of weld supports a ton of steel, the gaffer says.
They're welding up long ramps to carry army trucks.
(Within a year they will be used at Remagen, to cross the Rhine)
Today has started well, no raids last night, no rain.

The steel is dry and clean.
The dark glass in their visors turns the sun to green,
but when their eyes are on the job, it means
that as they get *a strike* they won't go snow-blind.

Watch the flux and weld start fizzing at the join.
It peppers tiny seeds with comet tails, bursts of dodgem
crackle, gold spider sparkler lights. A moment of gold jam,
when cold, the slag's buffed off to leave a shining silver seam.

Dot says 'It's good to use
your hands, although I'm fubsy in these gloves.
'Cos when the clamp's in place, you're part of it,
the arc, the contact made, the feel of fusing things.

Best bit? Unrationed grub at the canteen, I eat
my fill. Our permits let us nip across the bridge at night -
Fridays, we meet the Yanks. Treat us royal, them, they like to pay.
Tonight the pictures, I'm in love with Laurence Olivier.'

v   *Who Goes There?*

voices   We, the all-nighters, paramedics, late-night drivers,
        late shift and early workers, walkers, runners,
        writers going without sleep… reporters,
        lyricists and balladeers, storytellers, letter-writers,
        lovers, slow…. who view the Thames at night without despair.

voice   *'And we have seen night lifted in thine arms,*
        The city's fiery parcels all undone…
        Under thy shadow by the piers I waited'……

voice   Wasn't it Sam Weller says to Pickwick
        I had *"unfurnished lodgins' for a fortnight"*
        beneath the arches of that old bridge?

voice   Yes, Dickens knew about the down and outs.
        Beside the tollbooth's brazier, he sat with 'Pea',
        the night patrol, keeping a list of those hooked free;
        for every one they saved, two washed
        into the river. Fallen women, falling men.

voice   *'sweet Thames run softly till I end my song'*

voice   At Waterloo they lifted Heather up
        the night the *Marchioness* went down.
        Unwelcome on the oily river bed
        she was spat out three times, winded,
        thrust at snarling concrete curs,
        the current flinging her upstream.

voices   Still the night watch, still a toll, despite deliverers…
        mid-riverers who know the water well, its swell,
        debris and smells.

& even now the Lifeboat crew is mustering,
alarms are ringing on the deck, the river black
as coffee, lamps tangerines.

Four board the rib…. are off,
already past Blackfriars, leaving a lace of wash
to loop round *Harmony*, the pleasure boat
at a pontoon which bears the sign:
PLEASE EASE DOWN   MEN AT WORK

and every dark tower's long reflection in the river's mirror
shakes dark blue; red eyes of scattered port lights bob.

Dead calm again, a gull salutes two cormorants, a pigeon swoops.
Cranes pull out the pins and plumes worn in their hats of night.

Tattered twilight falls apart,
the Thames is swept, the city's smeared faces cleansed.

Streetlights shut off, the lifeboat sputters back,
no urgency, but there's a new insistence, sunrise.

VI   *Song of Sunrise*

Behind that word is unrise, slugabed, stay put, no, no I'll not get up.
Days not to act. Days when you must. The morning comes…

Perhaps the perfect morning when the air's a ruffled field, light multiplies
and blooms, a meadow stretching on the river's face.

Perhaps the sirens' *meadow starred with flowers* where, Circe
warned, *enchanting song* would mesmerise the crew and Ulysses.

Steer clear, she tells him, stuff your ears. Wrap your head.
For if their voices lure you in, you won't get home.

In Homer, sirens were two daughters of a river god,
who rose up with the mist and called

Come to our river bed
In mist that coils from the water like an eel.

Perhaps they called the teenage girl to join them
after sunrise last July. Perhaps they sang to Karen,

twenty one, waking in a bash with Gareth and the dog.
Evenings on the bridge she'd sell herself, never begged.

Sometimes she would blow two quid
on cornflowers, her kind of blue.

Perhaps a patient in the Sleep Room at the Royal Waterloo
would hear the sirens hum a childhood tune.

Perhaps they swam beside the kids in the inflatable
who whizzed upriver with their Dad waving a big flag

protesting we are 'IN'; only days
before Jo Cox, their mother, died....

Perhaps they comforted a woman huddled on the steps,
beside the small blue swallow tiles, cadging cigarettes.

Perhaps my father heard them
on his last uncertain walk across the Thames

remembering Admiralty interviews. I think their song
reminded him how ocean whitens as it turns to meet the sun.

Perhaps you also know the song they sing at sunrise.
Perhaps we all know someone they have called.

Oh ladies, ladies. Morning light, leaves, flowers on the banks,
the promises you meant for us.

LAST DAY AT THE SAVOY

after James McNeill Whistler's lithograph of his wife, Beatrice,
By the Balcony, 1896

Would you send the maid away, Jimmy,
               and sing your Russian hymn?
                                  I liked that, love.
        Yes, one verse was enough.

Tell me –
        the little cabman, is he there
with his grey horse – waiting –
               at the railing round the grass?

Recall, would you recall for me how good
things smell?
               Baking in the Rue du Bac… I cannot quite
                                      remember

And those two pigeons never leave –
               you must be keeping them in crumbs,
immortals on our balcony.
                            Look after them

The river mist is closing in …
I think I see
        a thumbprint on the sky.
                    Is that the old night's moon?

When it was light I dreamed
                     you hailed a painted boat
             out on the Thames, a boat
                 to row me home
                         upstream

NOTES

Locomotion of Laundry: the term Locomotion was coined by Sir Thomas Browne.

Flag: every day for forty years Despina Achladioti, the sole remaining islander on Rho, flew Greece's colours in defiance of Turkish authorities who claimed the island was in Turkish waters. She died alone in 1982 and was buried on the island with full military honours.

The Queen of Naples refers to *The Tempest* and to a treatise on beekeeping by Charles Butler, *The Feminine Monarchie*, first published by Joseph Barnes, Oxford, in 1609.

After the Frontier, 'the Golden Road to Samarkand' recalls a line from the verse play *Hassan* by James Elroy Flecker which opened in London in 1923. When the Third Afghan War was resolved in late 1923, wives were permitted to join members of the British Legation in Kabul for the first time.

First Flower of the Day takes some lines from Pierre de Ronsard's poem "Mignonne, allons voir si la rose", 1545 (let us see if the rose who showed off her dress of purple to the sun this morning...) and Donne's 'A Valediction Forbidding Mourning', c.1611.

A Piece of Chalk is written after an essay on the colour white by G.K. Chesterton, *The Daily News*, (London) November 4, 1905.

Waterloo Sunrise: in Part II, Monet's letter is borrowed from Richard Kendall (ed.) *Monet by Himself: Paintings, Drawings, Pastels, Letters* (London: Macdonald Orbis, 1989) translated by Bridget Strevens Marzo. In Part V, 'And we have seen night' is from Hart Crane's *The Bridge*, 'Sweet Thames' from Edmund Spenser's *Prothalamion.* In part VI, lines from Homer's Odyssey Book 12 are translated by Robert Fagles.

ACKNOWLEDGEMENTS

Thanks are due to the editors of the following publications in which poems first appeared: *Ambit, Best British Poetry* (2013), *Morley Review, New Walk, New Welsh Review, Not Very Quiet, Poetry on the Lake, Salzburg Poetry Review, Shearsman, Southword, Stand, The London Magazine, Times Literary Supplement.*

'Keepers of the States of Sleep and Wakefulness' was recorded in the time of Covid-19 in April 2020 and made into a short film by Jack Trewin with music by Musica Donum Dei. While celebrating the eight named nurses, night staff at Kings College Hospital, I dedicate the YouTube recording to all NHS nurses.

'*A Piece of Chalk*' was commissioned for Winchester Poetry Festival's *Chalk Poets; New Poetry from the South Downs* (2016) ed. by Stephanie Norgate and published by South Downs National Parks Authority.

'Reach', after John Corigliano's *Elegy* (second movement of his Concerto for Clarinet and Orchestra, 1977) was commissioned for Hear Hear (2008), a listening collaboration between Royal Academy of Music and Goldsmiths College.

'Waterloo Sunrise' was commissioned for the Waterloo Festival 2017 and first performed at the church of St John's, Waterloo on 16 June 2017. With its proem, its own trailer, it reappears in the essay 'Light Over Water' in *Riverine: Architecture and Rivers,* eds. G. Adler and M. Guerci, Routledge (2018).

I have drawn on radio transcripts by Muriel D. Miller, born in India, United Provinces, now Uttar Pradesh, in 1896. Her broadcasts for the BBC, made in the period following Partition, include *Living in Afghanistan*, Woman's Hour, 8 December 1947; *White Child in India*, Children's Hour, 10 June 1948; *The Kabul Road*, Children's Hour, 1 November 1948; *Bazaars*, Children's Hour, 27 June 1949; *From Lahore to Bucharest*, Children's Hour, 12 February 1951; *London Calling London*, Eastern Service, 7 March 1951; *Buried Treasure in the Zemindari*, Children's Hour, 30 September 1955; *My First Remembered Christmas*, Children's Hour, 23 December 1955. Among her papers are also her unpublished memoirs: *Half A Lifetime* (1951) and *Judy's Indian Childhood*, entrusted to me at her death in 1994.